JEWELRY PHOTOGRAPHY & ETSY LISTING T

Capture Stunning Photos and Write Product Descriptions That Sell

Wilfred Kent

Copyright © 2025 by [Wilfred Kent]

All rights reserved. No part of this publication may be reproduced, stored in a retrieval system, or transmitted in any form or by any means—electronic, mechanical, photocopying, recording, or otherwise—without the prior written permission of the publisher, except for brief quotations in printed reviews.

This book is intended for educational and recreational purposes only. The author and publisher have made every effort to ensure the accuracy and safety of the techniques described herein, but they assume no responsibility for errors, omissions, or any outcomes related to the use of the information or projects.

Table of Contents

- Chapter 1: Getting Started with Jewelry Photography 4
  - Overview 4
- Chapter 2: Defining Your Brand and Target Audience 9
  - Tools & Materials 9
- Chapter 3: Essential Photography Equipment 13
  - Tools & Materials 13
- Chapter 4: Budget-Friendly Studio Setup 19
- Chapter 5: Harnessing Natural Light 24
- Chapter 6: Mastering Artificial Lighting 28
- Chapter 7: Styling Backdrops and Props 33
- Chapter 8: Composition and Framing Techniques 38
- Chapter 9: Macro and Close-Up Photography 42
- Chapter 10: Post-Processing Workflow 51
- Chapter 11: Advanced Editing Techniques 55
- Chapter 12: Creating Branded Photo Templates 60
- Chapter 13: Crafting Effective Listing Titles and Tags 65
- Chapter 14: Writing Persuasive Product Descriptions 70
- Chapter 15: Etsy SEO and Keyword Research 74
- Chapter 16: Pricing Strategies and Inventory Planning 79
- Chapter 17: Shop Branding and Visual Identity 83
- Chapter 18: Promoting Your Listings on Social Media 88
- Chapter 19: Tracking Performance and Scaling Your Business 93
  - The end 98

Chapter 1: Getting Started with Jewelry Photography

Overview

Jewelry photography is the cornerstone of any successful online shop. Before a potential buyer reads your listing description or clicks "Add to Cart," they form their first impression through your images. In this chapter, you'll learn why mastering basic camera settings and preparing a simple workspace will immediately elevate the professionalism of your photos. By the end of this chapter, you'll be ready to plan and execute a small-scale jewelry shoot that yields crisp, well-lit, and accurate images—no expensive studio required.

Tools & Materials

To begin, gather these essentials. You don't need top-of-the-line gear; many sellers achieve stunning results with budget-friendly equipment and household items.

- **Camera** (DSLR or mirrorless preferred, but a high-end smartphone works too)
- **Macro lens** or macro attachment (for close-up detail shots)
- **Tripod** with adjustable head (stability is key to tack-sharp images)
- **Light source**
    - Natural: large window with diffused sunlight
    - Artificial: LED panels or inexpensive clamp lights with daylight-balanced bulbs
- **Diffuser and reflector**
    - DIY diffuser (white shower curtain, translucent paper)
    - Reflector (white foam board or silver card)
- **Backdrop**

- Plain surfaces: white foam core, black velvet, wood grain laminate

- **Cleaning supplies**
    - Microfiber cloths, jewelry brush, compressed air blower

- **Props and styling aids**
    - Jewelry stands, T-pins, museum wax for positioning

- **Computer and tethering cable** (optional for instant image review)

Step-by-Step Guide

Follow these concrete steps to set up and execute your first shoot. Adjust as needed for your space and budget.

1. **Define your shoot goals**
    - Decide which piece(s) to photograph and in what style (e.g., flat lay, on-model, detail shot).
    - Sketch a simple shot list: front view, angled view, close-up of clasp or texture.

2. **Prepare your workspace**
    - Choose a tabletop near a large window (north- or east-facing for soft light).
    - Clear clutter—your backdrop should occupy most of the frame.
    - Position tripod so camera sensor is parallel to the plane of the jewelry for even focus.

3. **Set up lighting**
    - If using natural light, diffuse direct sunlight with a sheer curtain or tracing paper.

- For artificial light, place two lights at roughly 45° angles on either side of the jewelry, with a diffuser between light and subject.

4. **Arrange your backdrop and props**
   - Smooth out fabric backdrops and secure edges with tape.
   - Position reflectors opposite each light source to fill shadows.
   - Mount rings or pendants on stands; for necklaces lay them in a gentle curve.

5. **Clean and position the jewelry**
   - Remove fingerprints or dust with a blower and microfiber cloth.
   - Use museum wax or T-pins to angle pieces so they catch light.
   - Check from camera's perspective that no unwanted reflections peek into the frame.

6. **Configure camera settings**
   - Switch to manual (M) or aperture-priority (A/AV) mode.
   - Set aperture between f/8 and f/16 for sufficient depth of field.
   - Choose ISO 100–200 to minimize noise.
   - Adjust shutter speed to achieve correct exposure (use a cable release or timer to avoid shake).

7. **Focus and compose**
   - Engage live view or magnified view to fine-tune focus on the most critical detail (stone facets, hallmarks).

- Apply the rule of thirds or center the piece, depending on your branding style.

8. **Take test shots and refine**
    - Review images on your computer or camera LCD.
    - Verify color accuracy, sharpness, and exposure.
    - Tweak lights, reflectors, or camera settings and shoot another test.

9. **Capture your final images**
    - Work through your shot list methodically.
    - Vary angles slightly to give yourself options in post-processing.

10. **Back up your files**
    - Immediately transfer RAW or high-resolution JPEG files to your computer.
    - Create a backup on an external drive or cloud storage.

Tips & Tricks

- **Keep consistency:** Use the same background, lighting angles, and camera height for all pieces in a given collection to maintain a cohesive shop aesthetic.

- **Control reflections:** Black foam or "flag" cards can block unwanted light sources and keep metal surfaces clean.

- **Experiment with height:** Small clear acrylic blocks or risers let you photograph multi-dimensional pieces from different perspectives.

- **Maintain camera stability:** Even on a tripod, use a remote shutter or two-second timer to eliminate vibration.

- **Use tethered shooting:** If possible, connect your camera to a computer via USB so you can evaluate images immediately at full size.

- **Label your shots:** Rename files on import (e.g., "Silver-Floral-Ring_Front.jpg") to streamline organization and later listing.

- **Practice patience:** Jewelry shoots often require fine adjustments—give yourself ample time, and don't rush the setup.

- **Keep a shoot journal:** Note settings and lighting positions that worked best; you'll build an efficient routine over time.

Chapter 2: Defining Your Brand and Target Audience

Tools & Materials

- **Brand workbook or journal** — to capture ideas, sketches, and notes

- **Mood board platform** (e.g., Pinterest, Canva) — for visual inspiration

- **Color-palette generator** (e.g., Coolors.co) — to select a cohesive scheme

- **Competitor audit sheet** — simple spreadsheet or table

- **Buyer-persona template** — fields for demographics, interests, pain points

- **Survey or feedback form** (Google Forms, Typeform) — to collect real-world insights

- **Notebook and pen** — for quick brainstorming anywhere

Step-by-Step Guide

1. **Brainstorm Your Brand Essence**

    - List three words that capture your jewelry's personality (elegant, bohemian, minimalist).

    - Note the emotions you want customers to feel when they see your pieces (confidence, nostalgia, joy).

2. **Assemble a Visual Mood Board**

    - Collect 15–20 images—photos, color swatches, textures—that reflect your style.

    - Look for consistent patterns: do you lean toward warm neutrals, bright jewel tones, or cool metallics?

    - Refine to your top 8–10 images to establish a clear visual vibe.

3. **Define Your Color Palette and Typography**
   - Use a palette tool to extract 3–5 primary and secondary colors from your mood board.
   - Choose one or two typefaces (serif vs. sans-serif) that match your aesthetic—e.g., classic serif for luxury, clean sans-serif for modern.

4. **Conduct a Competitor Audit**
   - Identify 5 Etsy shops with similar styles or price points.
   - For each, note their:
     - Profile photography style (lighting, backgrounds)
     - Listing tone (casual vs. formal)
     - Price range and bestseller types
   - Record strengths you admire and gaps you can fill.

5. **Build Buyer Personas**
   - Create 2–3 hypothetical customers, giving each:
     - Age range, gender, location
     - Income level or spending habits
     - Hobbies, values, preferred shopping channels
     - Biggest jewelry-related challenges (finding hypoallergenic pieces, gifting, self-treating)
   - Use real feedback from surveys or past customers whenever possible.

6. **Craft Your Brand Statement**

- Write one concise sentence:

  "At [Shop Name], we create [adjective] [jewelry type] for [persona] who want [benefit]."

- Example: "At Luna Links, we handcraft minimalist silver necklaces for urban professionals who value effortless elegance."

7. **Translate Brand into Photography Guidelines**

    - Decide on a consistent lighting style (soft, natural window light vs. crisp studio light).

    - Choose 1–2 backdrop textures (marble slab, linen cloth) that complement your color palette.

    - Select a consistent prop style—organic elements, geometric shapes, or none at all.

8. **Establish Listing Voice and Tone**

    - Align your description style with your brand:

        - Warm and conversational ("Wrap yourself in gentle moonlight…")

        - Polished and precise ("18K gold-plated chain, hypoallergenic stainless steel clasp").

    - Draft a sample opening sentence that you can adapt for all listings.

9. **Document Your Guidelines**

    - Compile your findings into a one-page "Brand Guide."

    - Include: brand statement, color codes (hex values), font names, photography do's & don'ts, sample description lines.

- Save as a PDF for quick reference before each shoot or listing session.

Tips & Tricks

- **Keep it simple:** A lean, 1–2-sentence brand statement is easier to remember and apply than lengthy mission statements.

- **Use free tools:** Canva's mood-board templates and Coolors' color wheels accelerate the creative process.

- **Validate with feedback:** Share your buyer personas and sample images with friends or past buyers to confirm you're on target.

- **Iterate over time:** Your brand will evolve—set a quarterly reminder to review and tweak your guide.

- **Stay authentic:** Don't chase every trend; focus on what genuinely reflects your design ethos and appeals to your customers.

- **Document each shoot's style notes:** Jot down lighting angles and prop placements that align with your brand guide so you can reproduce them consistently.

- **Bookmark competitor listings:** Keep a running list of three or four shops you admire for ongoing inspiration without copying.

- **Leverage analytics:** Once live, monitor which listings perform best and see how they align with your brand guidelines—refine accordingly.

Chapter 3: Essential Photography Equipment

Tools & Materials

- **Camera Body**
    - DSLR (e.g., Canon EOS Rebel series) or mirrorless (e.g., Sony α6000 series)
    - High-end smartphone (recent iPhone or Android flagship) with manual control apps

- **Lenses**
    - **Macro lens** (60–105 mm focal length, 1:1 magnification) for close-up detail
    - **Prime lens** (35 mm or 50 mm) for environmental shots or wider compositions
    - **Extension tubes** (budget alternative for macro work)

- **Tripod & Support**
    - Sturdy tripod with adjustable center column and ball head
    - **Macro focusing rail** (optional) for fine focus adjustments
    - **Remote shutter release** or camera timer function

- **Reflectors & Diffusers**
    - 5-in-1 collapsible reflector (white, silver, gold, black panels)
    - Translucent diffusion panel (folding fabric or DIY tracing-paper frame)

- **Backdrop & Props**
    - Foam-core boards (white and black)

- Textured boards (marble, wood-grain, slate)
- Clear acrylic blocks or jewelry risers

- **Lighting Accessories**
  - Continuous LED panels with adjustable brightness
  - Daylight-balanced bulbs (5,500–6,500 K) for clamp lights
  - Softboxes or DIY diffusion boxes

- **Storage & Power**
  - Fast memory cards (UHS-I U3 or higher)
  - Extra camera batteries
  - Cable management clips

- **Cleaning & Maintenance**
  - Air blower, soft-bristle brush, microfiber cloths
  - Lens-cleaning solution and tissues

Step-by-Step Guide

1. **Assess Your Budget and Needs**
   - Determine your monthly budget for photography upgrades.
   - Start with a reliable camera (even a recent smartphone) and upgrade gradually—lens before body.

2. **Choose the Right Camera**
   - For beginners, a mirrorless or DSLR with good low-ISO performance gives flexibility.

- If you shoot handheld or travel often, prioritize lighter mirrorless bodies.
- Ensure your camera supports manual exposure controls and RAW capture.

3. **Select the Optimal Macro Lens**
    - A 60 mm macro gives a working distance suitable for necklaces and bracelets.
    - A 100 mm macro provides more breathing room for capturing rings and delicate pieces.
    - If budget is tight, add extension tubes to your existing lens, but be mindful of slight image-quality loss.

4. **Stabilize with a Tripod**
    - Invest in a tripod rated for at least double your camera's weight.
    - A ball head allows quick angle adjustments, while a geared head offers precise movements.
    - Mount a macro focusing rail on the tripod for fine, incremental focus shifts.

5. **Gather Reflectors and Diffusers**
    - Use a white reflector to fill shadows softly; silver for stronger specular highlights.
    - Gold panels introduce warm accents—ideal for yellow gold pieces.
    - Position a diffuser between your light source and subject to soften harsh beams.

6. **Prepare Backdrops and Props**

- Keep three staple backdrops: white, black, and one textured surface that complements your brand palette.
- Use clear acrylic blocks to lift pieces off the backdrop, adding depth and reflection control.
- Try household items—marble tile, slate coasters, or wooden cutting boards—for unique textures.

7. **Optimize Lighting**

    - Place two continuous lights at 45° angles; use softboxes for even coverage.
    - Adjust brightness so your camera settings remain within ISO 100–200.
    - Balance natural and artificial sources by matching bulb color temperature to window light (~5,500 K).

8. **Organize Power and Storage**

    - Always carry two fully charged batteries and a fresh memory card.
    - Label cards with dates or shoot IDs to prevent mix-ups.
    - Use cable clips or hooks to keep cords out of the frame.

9. **Implement Cleaning Protocols**

    - Before each shoot, blow away dust, polish metals, and remove fingerprints with a microfiber cloth.
    - Clean your lens with a blower first, then lens tissue and solution for stubborn marks.
    - Store gear in protective cases to minimize maintenance.

10. **Test and Calibrate**

- Before your first shoot, bracket test exposures (e.g., ±1 stop) to verify dynamic range.
- Capture a color-checker target to profile your editing software later.
- Review test images on a calibrated monitor, making note of any shadows, reflections, or focus issues.

Tips & Tricks

- **Rent Before Buying:** Test high-end lenses or lights via local camera-rental services to ensure they fit your workflow.
- **Smartphone Hacks:** Clip-on macro lenses and light-diffusing phone cases can approximate professional setups at a fraction of the cost.
- **DIY Reflector Board:** Cover foam board with aluminum foil or white poster board to create an instant reflector.
- **Maintain Gear Logs:** Record serial numbers, purchase dates, and service history in a simple spreadsheet for insurance and warranty claims.
- **Cable Management:** Velcro straps or binder clips keep cords tidy and prevent accidental tugs during shoots.
- **Micro-Adjust Focus:** Some cameras allow autofocus micro-adjustments—fine-tune your lens for the sharpest detail.
- **Custom Backdrop Storage:** Roll fabric backdrops on PVC pipes and hang to avoid creases.
- **Bulk-Buy Supplies:** Stock up on cleaning wipes, batteries, and memory cards when you find a sale—turnaround time between shoots matters.

- **Regular Firmware Updates:** Check manufacturers' sites monthly to install firmware improvements that enhance performance and compatibility.
- **Label Lenses:** Mark settings (f-stop, focal length) on lens hoods with removable tape to speed repeated setups.

Chapter 4: Budget-Friendly Studio Setup

Tools & Materials

- **DIY Light Tent Frame Materials**
    - PVC pipes and connectors (½" or ¾")
    - White bridal veil fabric or shower curtain liner
    - Velcro strips or binder clips

- **Inexpensive Lighting Options**
    - Clamp-style LED work lights (daylight-balanced bulbs)
    - Desk lamps with flexible necks
    - Reflective Mylar emergency blankets (to amplify light)

- **Backdrop Supplies**
    - Foam-core poster boards (white, black, gray)
    - Vinyl shelf liner (wood-grain or marble print)
    - Wrapping paper or fabric remnants

- **Space-Saving Supports**
    - Folding table or collapsible desk
    - Stackable plastic crates or storage bins
    - Wall-mounted pegboard or shelving

- **Additional Accessories**
    - Painter's tape and removable command strips

- Binder clips, clothespins, or spring clamps
- Cardboard boxes (for diffuser and flag panels)
- Clear acrylic risers (optional but affordable online)
- Extension cords and power strips

Step-by-Step Guide

1. **Choose and Prepare Your Space**
   - Select a corner with access to power outlets.
   - Clear clutter and ensure flat, stable surfaces.
   - If natural light is available, orient your setup near a window with north- or east-facing exposure.

2. **Build a DIY Light Tent**
   - Assemble a PVC frame roughly 18″ × 18″ × 18″ (adjust size for larger pieces).
   - Drape the frame with translucent bridal veil fabric or a white shower curtain liner.
   - Secure fabric edges with Velcro or binder clips, leaving one side open for camera access.

3. **Set Up Inexpensive Lights**
   - Clamp two LED work lights to the tent's sides at 45° angles.
   - Fit each light with a daylight-balanced (5,500 K–6,000 K) bulb.
   - If lighting feels harsh, soften it by sandwiching a second layer of fabric or tracing paper between the bulb and tent wall.

4. **Create DIY Diffusers and Flags**

    o Cut cardboard panels and cover one side with white tissue paper for additional diffusion.

    o Use black poster board as "flags" to block unwanted reflections or shape light direction.

    o Attach panels with binder clips or tape onto the tent frame or light stands.

5. **Assemble Backdrops**

    o Use foam-core boards as flat surfaces—white for high-key looks, black for drama, gray for versatility.

    o Adhere vinyl shelf liner or wrapping paper onto foam core for textured backgrounds.

    o Prop boards vertically or lay them flat, depending on the shot style (standing vs. overhead).

6. **Optimize Limited Footprint**

    o Place your tent and lights on a folding table that can be tucked away when not in use.

    o Store stands, crates, and backdrops under the table or on a nearby shelf.

    o Mount a pegboard above the shooting area to hang clamps, reflectors, and small props for easy access.

7. **Organize Power and Cables**

    o Route extension cords behind your shooting table, secured with removable cable clips.

- Label each plug (e.g., "Left Light," "Right Light," "Camera Charger") for quick setup.
- Consider a power strip with surge protection to safeguard your equipment.

8. **Test Your Mini-Studio**
    - Position a piece of jewelry inside the tent and take test shots at various angles.
    - Check for even illumination and absence of harsh hot spots.
    - Adjust tent walls, diffusers, and flags until lighting appears soft and uniform.

9. **Fine-Tune Background Distance**
    - Experiment by moving the backdrop closer or farther from the jewelry to control shadows.
    - Closer backdrops yield crisp seamless looks; increased distance introduces subtle vignetting.

10. **Pack Down and Protect**
    - After shooting, collapse the PVC frame and fold fabric neatly.
    - Store flat backdrops upright in a wall slot or behind a door.
    - Keep lamps and lights in a labeled box to prevent bulb damage.

Tips & Tricks

- **Repurpose Household Items:** Use white foam-core from school supply stores; leftover gift wrap or fabric scraps make unique backdrops.

- **Budget Lighting:** Emergency blankets (Mylar) make excellent reflectors—cut and mount on cardboard for a silver surface.

- **Modular Setup:** Build multiple small frames in varying sizes so you can swap tents for rings, necklaces, or bracelets.

- **Clip-On Diffusers:** Clip translucent plastic file folders to lamp heads for quick diffusion when on the go.

- **Mobile Solution:** If space is extremely tight, mount lights on a rolling cart to wheel your mini-studio in and out of view.

- **Backdrop Storage Hack:** Slide foam-core boards between beds or behind couches to keep them pristine.

- **DIY Light-box Alternative:** Turn a cardboard box into a light box by cutting out three sides and replacing them with diffuser panels—no pipe fittings needed.

- **Consistent Color:** Line the interior of your tent with neutral gray poster board to minimize color casts.

- **Multiple Uses:** Your PVC frame can double as a prop display—hang chains or earrings for quick styling.

- **Routine Maintenance:** Wipe diffusers and tent fabric gently after each session to prevent dust buildup and maintain light quality.

Chapter 5: Harnessing Natural Light

Tools & Materials

- **Window or glass door** with ample daylight (north- or east-facing preferred)
- **Sheer curtain or tracing paper** (for diffusion)
- **White foam-core board** or poster board (for reflectors)
- **Silver- or gold-foil card** (optional for accent highlights)
- **Adjustable stool or small table** (to position jewelry at window height)
- **Tripod** (for stability when shooting with slower shutter speeds)
- **Clamp or suction-cup hook** (to hang lightweight backdrops or diffusers)
- **White poster board or cardboard** (to serve as a base or shooting platform)

Step-by-Step Guide

1. **Select Your Window and Time of Day**
   - Aim for early morning (8–10 AM) or late afternoon (3–5 PM) when light is softest.
   - North-facing windows provide consistent, indirect light all day; east- and west-facing offer warmer tones at sunrise and sunset.

2. **Diffuse Direct Sunlight**
   - Hang a sheer curtain or stretch tracing paper across the window frame to scatter harsh rays.
   - Secure with removable hooks or binder clips, ensuring the entire pane is covered for uniform diffusion.

3. **Position Your Jewelry**

- Place a small table or stool 1–2 feet from the window, parallel to the window plane.
- Arrange your jewelry on a flat foam-core board or a backdrop that sits on the table.
- Angle the piece slightly toward the window to catch soft highlights on metal and stones.

4. **Use Reflectors to Fill Shadows**
    - Hold or prop a white poster board opposite the window to bounce light back onto the jewelry.
    - For stronger accent light, swap in a silver-foil card; for warmer fill, use gold-foil.
    - Adjust reflector distance: closer for intense fill, farther for subtle softening.

5. **Set Up Your Camera**
    - Mount on tripod to prevent blur at slower shutter speeds (e.g., 1/60 sec or slower).
    - Use aperture-priority mode (f/8–f/16) to maintain depth of field; let the camera select shutter speed.
    - Set ISO to 100–200 to keep noise low; raise only if absolutely necessary.

6. **Compose and Focus**
    - Frame your jewelry so the most eye-catching angle faces the window.
    - Use live-view zoomed in to manually focus on the critical element (gemstone facets, clasp details).

- Experiment with slight camera height changes—shoot from table height for flat lays or lower for angled depth.

7. **Capture Test Shots**
   - Take bracketed exposures (±1 EV) to ensure you capture the full tonal range.
   - Review on-camera histogram: aim for even distribution without clipping highlights or blacks.

8. **Fine-Tune and Shoot**
   - Move reflector or diffuser to eliminate unwanted shadows or glare.
   - Adjust window covering density (double up sheers) for extra softness if highlights look harsh.
   - Capture multiple angles: straight-on, 45°, and overhead to build your shot library.

9. **Store and Label Images**
   - Immediately back up files and label with lighting notes (e.g., "NorthWindow_AM8_f/11").
   - Record which reflector types and positions yielded best results for future reference.

Tips & Tricks

- **Cloudy-Day Advantage:** Overcast skies act as a giant softbox, yielding even light without additional diffusion.
- **Portable Diffuser Hack:** Clip a white silicone baking mat or translucent plastic folder over the window for quick diffusion on the go.

- **DIY Reflector Surfaces:** Aluminum foil over cardboard makes an economical silver reflector; flip to the cardboard side for neutral fill.

- **Watch for Color Casts:** If your window has tinted glass, place a color-checker card in the frame to correct during editing.

- **Minimize Glare:** Tilt the jewelry slightly away from the window if specular highlights become too intense.

- **Create a Light Tunnel:** Use foam-core boards on three sides of the jewelry to channel light in a U-shape, isolating the piece from ambient room light.

- **Record Your Setup:** Sketch a quick diagram of window position, reflector angles, and diffuser placement so you can replicate perfect shots.

- **Leverage Early-Morning Light:** Sunrise light through east-facing windows produces warm, directional light ideal for gold and warm-tone gemstones.

- **Use a Polarizing Filter:** A circular polarizer on your lens can cut unwanted reflections on metal and glass surfaces.

- **Clean Window & Background:** Wipe down the window pane and foam-core board before each shoot to avoid dust spots showing up in images.

Chapter 6: Mastering Artificial Lighting

Overview

While natural light can be beautiful, artificial lighting gives you total control over every aspect of your jewelry photos—day or night. Continuous LED panels and studio strobes each have strengths: LEDs allow real-time preview of shadows and highlights, strobes freeze motion and pack more power. In this chapter, you'll learn how to choose between these light types, position softboxes and modifiers for even illumination, and fine-tune your setup to deliver consistent, repeatable results for every shoot.

Tools & Materials

- **Continuous Lighting**
    - LED panels or bulbs (daylight-balanced, 5,500–6,500 K)
    - Desk lamps or clamp lights with adjustable heads

- **Strobe Lighting**
    - Monolights or pack-and-head systems
    - Light triggers or sync cables

- **Light Modifiers**
    - Softboxes (small to medium sizes, e.g., 12″×16″ to 24″×36″)
    - Umbrellas (shoot-through and reflective types)
    - Beauty dish or octabox (for specular highlights)
    - Grids, snoots, and barn doors (to shape and control spill)

- **Supporting Gear**
    - Light stands (rated for your lights' weight)

- Boom arm (for overhead shots)
- Color gels (for creative color fills)

- **Reflectors & Flags**
  - 5-in-1 reflector disc (white, silver, gold, black, translucent)
  - Foam-core flags (to cut light)

- **Accessories**
  - Power strips with surge protection
  - Cable clips and sandbags (for safety and stability)
  - Light meter (optional, for precise exposure)

Step-by-Step Guide

1. **Decide on Light Type**
   - Use continuous LEDs for quick setups, straightforward adjustments, and real-time feedback.
   - Choose strobes when you need higher output, faster recycle times, and sharper freeze of tiny movements (e.g., falling glitter).

2. **Set Your Color Temperature**
   - For LEDs and strobes with variable outputs, dial in 5,500 K to match daylight.
   - If mixing continuous and strobe, gel one source to match the other for consistent white balance.

3. **Position Key Light**

- Mount your main light (softbox or umbrella) at a 45° angle above and to one side of the jewelry.
- Aim slightly downward so light grazes the piece, accentuating textures and facets.

4. **Add Fill Light**

   - Opposite the key, place a secondary light at lower power or use a white reflector to soften shadows.
   - Adjust fill-to-key ratio (start at –1 stop under key) for desirable contrast.

5. **Control Light Spill**

   - Attach grids or barn doors to your key light to narrow its beam and prevent unwanted background illumination.
   - Use black flags to block stray rays from hitting reflective surfaces.

6. **Incorporate Back or Hair Light**

   - Position a small strobe or LED behind the jewelry, aimed at the background or rim of the piece.
   - Use a snoot or grid for a subtle glow that separates your jewelry from the backdrop.

7. **Fine-Tune with a Light Meter**

   - If available, meter each light at the jewelry's plane for precise exposure ratios.
   - Adjust power or distance to achieve target readings (e.g., f/11 at ISO 100, 1/160 sec).

8. **Test and Adjust**
   - Take test shots, then review on a calibrated monitor or camera LCD.
   - Look for blown highlights on metal and crushed blacks; tweak power, modifiers, or angles accordingly.

9. **Experiment with Modifiers**
   - Swap a softbox for an octabox to sharpen specular highlights on gemstones.
   - Try a baldric-style beauty dish for a controlled wraparound light that flatters polished surfaces.

10. **Lock In and Label**
    - Document stand heights, light angles, and modifier types in a simple diagram or spreadsheet.
    - Label stands and cables to recreate the exact setup in future sessions.

Tips & Tricks

- **TTL vs. Manual:** Use TTL (through-the-lens metering) for fast, automatic exposures; switch to manual mode for consistent output when you've dialed in your ideal settings.

- **Mixing Light Types:** When combining LEDs and strobes, gel strobes with CTO/CTB gels to match color temperatures.

- **DIY Barn Doors:** Cut stiff black poster board into flaps and tape onto softbox edges for custom light shaping.

- **Low-Power Fill:** Bounce strobe light into a white umbrella instead of using a second flash unit for more economical fill.

- **Bounce Cards:** Attach small white cards inside umbrellas to reflect some strobe light back toward the piece, reducing hotspots.

- **Distance Controls Power:** Remember that light intensity falls off by the inverse-square law—doubling the distance cuts output by roughly four stops.

- **Grid Patterns:** Use tighter grids (20°) for pinpoint highlights on rings; looser grids (40°) for even rim lighting on larger necklaces.

- **Safety First:** Sandbag each light stand and keep cables taped down to prevent trips or spills near valuable jewelry.

- **Consistent Refresh:** Run routine tests before each shoot day, especially if you've moved or swapped any modifiers.

- **Label Gels:** Write gel colors and densities on painter's tape and stick to the gel frame—saves time when recreating creative looks.

Chapter 7: Styling Backdrops and Props

Overview

A well-chosen backdrop and thoughtfully placed props can transform a simple jewelry image into an evocative scene that tells your brand's story. The right textures, colors, and complementary objects draw the eye to your piece and help convey its style—whether that's rustic boho, modern minimalism, or vintage romance. This chapter shows you how to select, prepare, and arrange backdrops and props to enhance your jewelry's appeal and strengthen your shop's visual identity.

Tools & Materials

- **Backdrop Surfaces**
    - Foam-core boards (neutral white, black, gray)
    - Textured sheets (marble contact paper, wood-grain vinyl)
    - Fabric swatches (linen, velvet, burlap)

- **Props and Styling Aids**
    - Natural elements (dried flowers, small branches, stones)
    - Geometric props (acrylic blocks, metal stands, ceramic dishes)
    - Lifestyle items (books, candles, coffee cups)
    - Jewelry display tools (T-pins, museum wax, neck busts)

- **Adhesives & Fasteners**
    - Museum putty or tack
    - Double-sided tape (removable)
    - Small clamps and clips

- **Color and Texture Accents**
    - Paper or fabric swatches in your brand palette
    - Decorative papers (watercolor sheets, handmade paper)
- **Preparation Supplies**
    - Microfiber cloths (for cleaning backdrops and props)
    - Painter's tape (for temporary placement)
    - Scissors and rotary cutter

Step-by-Step Guide

1. **Define Your Scene Concept**
    - Refer to your brand guide (Chapter 2) for color palette and mood keywords.
    - Choose a theme—e.g., beachy boho with driftwood and sand accents, or luxe minimal with marble and brass.

2. **Select the Base Backdrop**
    - Lay down a neutral foam-core for clean looks or a textured vinyl for character.
    - Smooth fabric backdrops over a board and secure edges with painter's tape to eliminate wrinkles.

3. **Gather Complementary Props**
    - Limit to 2–3 prop types to avoid visual clutter (e.g., one natural element, one geometric accent).
    - Ensure props share tonal harmony with your jewelry (warm woods for gold; cool stones for silver).

4. **Arrange Your Jewelry Display**

    - Position the piece using T-pins or museum wax to achieve the desired angle.
    - Consider using neck busts or ring cones to showcase hanging or elevated pieces.

5. **Position Props Around the Subject**

    - Group props asymmetrically to frame the jewelry and guide the viewer's gaze.
    - Keep negative space around the piece to prevent distractions.

6. **Layer Textures and Heights**

    - Place a small stack of books or acrylic risers to create multi-level interest.
    - Drape a folded fabric swatch behind or beneath the jewelry for subtle depth.

7. **Test Composition and Balance**

    - Shoot a quick overhead or 45° angle to evaluate balance between jewelry and props.
    - Adjust spacing—move props closer or farther away so the jewelry remains focal.

8. **Fine-Tune Color and Contrast**

    - Swap props or backdrops if colors compete with gemstone hues or metal finishes.
    - Use a small reflector to bounce light into shadowed areas without disturbing styling.

9. **Capture and Review**
    - Take several shots with slight variations—move a flower petal or rotate a ring by a few degrees.
    - Review on-screen to ensure no prop edges creep into the frame unintentionally.

10. **Document Your Setup**
    - Photograph your styled scene from above, noting prop placement and backdrop choice.
    - Save these reference shots alongside your shoot notes for consistent future recreation.

Tips & Tricks

- **Keep It Simple:** Less is more—focus attention on your jewelry by limiting props to accent, not overwhelm.

- **Scale Matters:** Match prop sizes proportionally to your jewelry—tiny pebbles work for rings, larger objects suit necklaces.

- **Color Cohesion:** Use props within one to two tones of your brand palette; avoid bright primary colors that pull focus.

- **Texture Contrast:** Pair smooth surfaces (glass, metal) with rough textures (wood, linen) to highlight material differences.

- **Use Negative Space:** Allow breathing room around your piece so it doesn't get lost among props.

- **Rotate Props:** Slightly tilt plates or blocks to introduce dynamic lines and guide the viewer's eye.

- **Layer Transparencies:** Place a clear acrylic block over a textured background to isolate the jewelry visually.

- **Seasonal Themes:** Swap in mini props—pine cones for winter, blossoms for spring—to keep your shop fresh and timely.

- **DIY Paint:** Paint inexpensive foam-core with subtle speckles or watercolor washes for unique, custom backgrounds.

- **Prop Storage:** Keep frequently used items organized in clear bins, labeled by material or color, for quick shoot prep.

Chapter 8: Composition and Framing Techniques

Overview

Effective composition transforms a simple jewelry snapshot into a compelling visual story. By applying classic photographic principles—such as the rule of thirds, leading lines, and strategic use of negative space—you guide the viewer's eye toward your piece's most captivating features. Thoughtful framing also ensures that color, shape, and texture are showcased in harmony with your brand aesthetic. In this chapter, you'll learn how to compose images that feel balanced, dynamic, and instantly attention-grabbing, whether you're shooting a delicate ring or a statement necklace.

Tools & Materials

- **Camera or smartphone** with grid overlay enabled
- **Tripod** with adjustable tilt to maintain consistent framing
- **Level or spirit bubble** (built into many tripod heads)
- **Marking tape or chalk** (for positioning items on flat-lay setups)
- **Live-view display or tethered monitor** (to review composition in real time)
- **Simple props for lines and shapes** (e.g., thread spools, wooden rulers, wires)
- **Backdrop with subtle texture or pattern** (to reinforce lines without distraction)

Step-by-Step Guide

1. **Enable Your Grid**

   Activate a 3×3 grid overlay in your camera or smartphone settings. This visual framework helps you align points of interest along imaginary intersections rather than in the dead center.

2. **Apply the Rule of Thirds**

3. Position key elements—gemstone, focal angle, clasp detail—near one of the four grid intersections. This off-center placement creates a sense of movement and natural balance.

4. **Incorporate Leading Lines**

   Use props or background elements (e.g., the edge of a textured board or a length of chain) to draw the viewer's gaze toward the jewelry's main feature. Ensure these lines converge gently at your focal point without overpowering it.

5. **Leverage Negative Space**

   Allow ample uncluttered area around your piece—especially in flat-lay shots—so the jewelry stands out crisply. Negative space also provides room for on-image text overlays or watermark placement when marketing on social media.

6. **Experiment with Symmetry and Centering**

   For pairs (earrings) or perfectly round objects (rings), center your subject against a simple backdrop. Symmetrical compositions evoke elegance and stability, ideal for luxury pieces.

7. **Vary Your Vantage Point**

   Alternate between straight-on, 45°, and overhead angles to discover the most flattering perspective. Slight shifts in camera height or tilt can dramatically change how facets catch the light.

8. **Frame with Natural Elements**

   Place simple, unobtrusive items—like a sprig of eucalyptus or a loop of chain—just outside the main subject area to "frame" your piece organically and add depth.

9. **Balance Color and Contrast**

10. If your jewelry has strong color (emeralds, sapphires), leave adjacent grid cells empty or in neutral tones to let the color pop. Conversely, use a dark backdrop behind light-colored metals to maximize contrast.

11. **Check Alignment and Horizon**

    Especially in angled shots, ensure horizontal lines (table edges, backdrop seams) sit level with the frame. A crooked horizon can distract and undermine the perceived quality of your work.

12. **Capture Multiple Crops**

    After your primary shot, zoom in for a tight crop on details and zoom out for environmental context. Save both for use in listings, social media, and promotional materials.

Tips & Tricks

- **Rule of Odds:** When styling multiple items, group them in odd numbers (three rings, five earrings) to create a more engaging visual rhythm.

- **Diagonal Dynamics:** Placing your piece on a gentle diagonal across the frame can increase dynamism and draw the viewer's eye along a natural path.

- **Center of Interest:** For pieces with a single standout feature (e.g., a large center stone), use the "golden spiral" approach—align the spiral's curve so it sweeps toward that feature.

- **Fill the Frame:** Don't hesitate to allow your jewelry to extend to the frame's edge for a bold, immersive look—just be mindful of cutting off important details.

- **Mirror Reflections:** Capture subtle reflections by placing your piece on a glossy surface; frame the shot low to include the mirrored image for a high-end feel.

- **Framing with Props:** Use negative-space props (e.g., open book pages, ceramic bowls) as partial borders, but keep them muted in color.

- **Subtle Cropping Guides:** If you shoot tethered, overlay simple crop templates (1:1, 4:5, 16:9) on your monitor to see how different aspect ratios will translate on various platforms.

- **Avoid Centered Eyes:** When photographing pieces meant to frame the face (earrings, pendants), leave generous headroom above or space to the side for model imagery or future marketing overlays.

- **Dynamic Compositions for Sets:** When showcasing matching sets, consider an "L" or "V" arrangement instead of a straight line to maintain viewer interest.

- **Review on Multiple Devices:** After shooting, preview your compositions on a phone, tablet, and monitor to ensure they read well at all sizes and aspect ratios.

Chapter 9: Macro and Close-Up Photography

Overview

Macro photography reveals the intricate beauty of jewelry—every facet, texture, and engraving becomes a visual jewel in itself. By using dedicated macro lenses (or macro attachments) and techniques like focus stacking, you'll capture razor-sharp detail that draws buyers in and conveys true craftsmanship. This chapter guides you through selecting the right tools, configuring your camera, and compositing multiple frames for gallery-worthy close-ups.

Tools & Materials

- **Macro Lens** (60–105 mm, 1:1 magnification)
- **Extension Tubes** (as budget alternative to a dedicated macro lens)
- **Macro Focusing Rail** (for precise, incremental focus shifts)
- **Tripod** with geared head or focusing rail mount
- **Remote Shutter Release** or camera timer
- **Continuous LED Light Panels** or ring light (for shadow-free illumination)
- **Reflector** (white or silver collapsible disc)
- **Diffuser** (tracing paper, sheer fabric)
- **Clamps, Museum Wax, T-Pins** (to secure and position small pieces)
- **Computer with Focus-Stacking Software** (e.g., Helicon Focus, Photoshop)

Step-by-Step Guide

1. **Mount and Level**

- Secure your camera on a sturdy tripod equipped with a geared head or focusing rail.
- Ensure the camera sensor is parallel to the jewelry plane to maintain even depth of field.

2. **Select Your ISO and Aperture**
   - Set ISO to 100–200 for minimal noise.
   - Choose a mid-range aperture (f/8–f/11) to balance depth of field with diffraction control.

3. **Position Lighting**
   - Use continuous LED panels or a ring light around the lens to minimize shadows.
   - Diffuse each light source through tracing paper or sheer fabric for soft, even coverage.

4. **Compose Your Shot**
   - Zoom in to frame the most intricate feature—stone facets, metal engraving, filigree.
   - Leave small margins for cropping after stacking.

5. **Fine-Tune Focus**
   - Switch to live-view magnified mode.
   - Start by focusing on the nearest point of interest (front facet or edge).

6. **Capture Focus-Stacked Sequence**

- Using the focusing rail, shift the camera forward or backward by small increments (1–2 mm).
- At each position, trigger the shutter remotely to avoid camera shake.
- Capture 10–20 frames spanning the full depth of the piece.

7. **Import and Stack**
    - Load the image sequence into focus-stacking software.
    - Let the program align and blend sharp areas from each frame into one composite.

8. **Review and Refine**
    - Inspect the stacked image at 100% zoom for artifacts or misaligned areas.
    - Mask or clone-stamp any glitches in Photoshop for a flawless finish.

9. **Color and Contrast Adjustments**
    - Correct white balance using a color-checker shot from the same session.
    - Fine-tune exposure, clarity, and highlights to bring out texture without introducing noise.

10. **Export High-Resolution Files**
    - Save as high-quality TIFF or maximum-quality JPEG for use in listings and marketing.
    - Rename files descriptively (e.g., "Emerald-Ring-CloseUp.tif") and back up immediately.

Tips & Tricks

- **Stable Environment:** Eliminate air currents and vibrations by closing windows and working on a solid surface.

- **Manual Focus Override:** Some lenses allow micro-focus adjustments—use these to refine before each stack.

- **Use a Bubble Level:** Built-in tripod head levels prevent tilt, keeping each focus slice consistent.

- **Limit Reflections:** Matte black flags or foam-core cutouts placed near edges can block stray highlights.

- **Variable Step Sizes:** For very convex pieces (domed stones), increase rail movement incrementally to cover depth.

- **Bracket Exposures:** If lighting is uneven, shoot bracketed sequences at –1, 0, +1 EV and stack each set for HDR sharpness.

- **Test with a Sample:** Practice on a spare piece or prop object (e.g., textured button) to dial in step size and lighting.

- **Automate with Tethering:** Some software and cameras support auto-stacking triggers—explore plugins or camera firmware.

- **Masking Mastery:** In post, use layer masks to manually blend any soft edges for perfect sharpness.

- **Sharpen Selectively:** Apply sharpening only to focal areas to avoid exaggerating noise in backgrounds.

Chapter 10: Color Accuracy and White Balance

Overview

Accurate color reproduction is essential in jewelry photography—buyers rely on your images to assess metal tones, gemstone hues, and overall craftsmanship. If your photos skew too warm or cool, you risk returns, disappointed customers, or diminished trust. In this chapter, you'll learn how to set a custom white balance in camera, use color-reference cards during your shoot, and calibrate your monitor so that what you see on screen matches the final product. Mastering these techniques ensures your listings display true-to-life colors across devices and platforms.

Tools & Materials

- **Gray or White Reference Card**
    - A neutral 18% gray card (for custom in-camera white balance)
    - A white balance target or gray patch on a color checker

- **Color-Checker Chart**
    - Standard 24- or 18-patch color chart (e.g., X-Rite ColorChecker Passport)

- **Monitor Calibration Device**
    - Hardware colorimeter or spectrophotometer (e.g., Datacolor Spyder, X-Rite i1Display)

- **RAW-Capable Camera**
    - DSLR, mirrorless, or smartphone with RAW mode (to preserve color data)

- **Tethering Software (Optional)**
    - Software that displays live images on a calibrated monitor during capture

- **Photo-Editing Software**

- Lightroom, Capture One, or Photoshop (for white balance adjustment and profile creation)

Step-by-Step Guide

1. **Set Up Your Color-Checker**

   Position your color-checker chart or gray card directly in the light path alongside your jewelry. Ensure it lies in the same plane and receives the same lighting.

2. **Capture a Reference Shot**

   In RAW mode, photograph the card or chart—this reference will guide both in-camera white balance and post-processing profiles.

3. **Customize In-Camera White Balance**

   - Switch your camera to custom white-balance mode.
   - Select the reference image of the gray card.
   - Confirm the camera reads the card and applies a neutral white balance for subsequent shots.

4. **Shoot Your Jewelry Images**

   - Keep the gray card in the frame for the first few shots, then remove it once white balance is locked.
   - Continue shooting in RAW to retain maximum color information.

5. **Import and Assign Profiles**

   - In Lightroom or Capture One, import your RAW files and reference shots.
   - Create a custom camera profile using the color-checker chart image (many tools automate this).

- Apply the profile to your jewelry images to ensure accurate baseline color.

6. **Fine-Tune White Balance in Post**
    - Use the eyedropper tool on the gray card preview to confirm neutrality.
    - Adjust temperature and tint sliders sparingly—relying on your calibrated profile reduces major shifts.

7. **Calibrate Your Monitor**
    - Install the calibration software and attach the colorimeter to your screen.
    - Follow the on-screen prompts to measure and adjust gamma, white point, and luminance.
    - Save and activate the new profile; your monitor will now display colors faithfully.

8. **Validate Across Devices**
    - Export test images and view them on a secondary device (phone, tablet).
    - Check that gemstone hues and metal finishes appear consistent—if not, review lighting and calibration.

9. **Embed Color Profiles on Export**
    - When exporting JPEGs or PNGs, embed the sRGB profile to standardize display on web and mobile devices.
    - Ensure export settings preserve color profile integrity and prevent unintended shifts.

10. **Maintain Routine Calibration**

- Schedule monitor recalibration monthly, or whenever ambient lighting in your workspace changes.
- Keep spare batteries for your colorimeter and store calibration files securely for reference.

Tips & Tricks

- **Avoid Mixed Lighting:** Turn off tungsten or fluorescent bulbs in your studio; stick to daylight-balanced sources to simplify white-balance control.

- **Use RAW Over JPEG:** RAW files retain full sensor data, making white-balance corrections more precise and less destructive.

- **Record Your Settings:** Keep a simple log of custom white-balance values and profiles used, so you can replicate exact conditions in future shoots.

- **Ambient Light Consistency:** Perform calibration and shooting under the same ambient light conditions—shifts in daylight or overhead lighting can throw off accuracy.

- **Soft Proofing:** In Photoshop, enable soft-proofing for web profiles (sRGB) to preview how colors will appear online.

- **ISO and Noise:** Higher ISO settings can introduce color noise; stick to ISO 100–200 when color fidelity is critical.

- **Spot Metering for Cards:** Use spot-metering mode on your camera to expose accurately for the gray card during your reference shot.

- **Backup Profiles:** Save your calibration profiles and camera profiles in multiple locations—reinstallation or computer upgrades shouldn't force you to redo months of work.

- **Check for Drift:** Occasionally verify your white-balance settings against a gray card mid-shoot, especially during long sessions or changing daylight.

- **Consistent Viewing Conditions:** Calibrate in the same lighting environment where you normally edit—avoid bright windows or overhead fluorescents during calibration.

Chapter 10: Post-Processing Workflow

Tools & Materials

- **Photo-Editing Software** (Adobe Lightroom Classic, Capture One, or Darktable)

- **RAW File Support** (ensure your software recognizes your camera's RAW format)

- **Computer with Adequate RAM and a Calibrated Monitor** (for smooth performance and accurate color)

- **External Hard Drive or Cloud Storage** (for fast backups)

- **Keyword and Metadata Template** (spreadsheet or software preset)

- **Custom Export Presets** (for web-optimized JPEGs and high-resolution archives)

Step-by-Step Guide

1. **Import with Consistent Settings**

    - Create an import preset that applies your custom camera profile, auto-applies lens corrections, and embeds metadata (copyright, creator name).

    - Enable "Build Previews" at medium or 1:1 size to speed up culling.

2. **Organize and Cull Efficiently**

    - Use star ratings or color labels to sort images at a glance—e.g., for keepers, 2★ for "maybe," 0★ for rejects.

    - Quickly scan thumbnails in grid view, flagging sharp, well-lit shots and rejecting out-of-focus or poorly composed frames.

3. **Keyword and Metadata Application**

- Apply descriptive keywords (metal type, gemstone, style) to keep files searchable.
- Use batch-apply metadata to tag season, collection name, and copyright info in one pass.

4. **Batch-Adjust Basic Exposure and Contrast**
    - Select your top 1★ images, then use "Auto Tone" as a baseline.
    - Adjust exposure, highlights, shadows, whites, and blacks as a group—fine-tune individual shots only if needed.

5. **Synchronize White Balance and Color Profiles**
    - Apply your custom white-balance setting created in Chapter 10 across the batch.
    - Sync any local adjustments (temperature, tint) so all images in a set share the same look.

6. **Lens Corrections and Transform**
    - Enable profile-based distortion and vignetting corrections for your lens.
    - Use guided upright or manual transform tools to straighten horizon lines and level your backgrounds.

7. **Crop and Straighten**
    - Apply consistent aspect ratios (1:1 for Instagram, 4:5 for Etsy) via saved crop overlays.
    - Straighten using grid overlays, ensuring backdrops and props sit level.

8. **Spot-Removal and Local Adjustments**

- Use spot-heal or clone tools to remove dust, lint, or small scratches.
- Employ radial or graduated filters sparingly to draw attention to the jewelry's focal point.

9. **Apply Sharpening and Noise Reduction**
    - Use a standard sharpening mask (e.g., Amount 70, Radius 1, Detail 25) on all images, adjusting based on resolution.
    - Apply noise reduction only if you've shot above ISO 200; preserve fine detail whenever possible.

10. **Export with Presets and Backup**
    - Export two sets: high-res TIFF or JPEG for archiving, and web-optimized JPEG (sRGB, quality 80) with your watermark if desired.
    - Name files descriptively and organize them into "Final" and "Archive" folders; immediately back up to external or cloud storage.

Tips & Tricks

- **Use Collections or Albums:** Group images by product or shoot date to keep projects separate and streamline batch edits.
- **Smart Previews:** In Lightroom, build Smart Previews to edit offline and save hard-drive space without sacrificing quality.
- **Auto-Sync with Keyboard Shortcut:** After perfecting one image, hit "Sync Settings" (or ⌘ + Shift + S) to apply edits to the entire selection.
- **Virtual Copies:** Create variants (e.g., white vs. black background) without duplicating raw files by using virtual copies.

- **Custom Keyboard Shortcuts:** Map your most-used adjustments (crop, spot heal, rating) to keys for lightning-fast editing.

- **Snapshot Workflow:** Save snapshots at key stages (imported, basic edit, final) so you can revert or compare versions quickly.

- **Backup Catalog Regularly:** Schedule monthly backups of your editing catalog and presets to avoid data loss.

- **Split-Screen Comparison:** Use side-by-side view to compare before and after, ensuring edits enhance rather than overprocess.

- **Watermarking Strategy:** If you watermark, place it consistently in a corner outside your Etsy thumbnail safe zone.

- **Stay Versioned:** When making major stylistic changes, duplicate the finished folder as "V2" to keep past images intact.

Chapter 11: Advanced Editing Techniques

Overview

Basic adjustments—exposure, contrast, and white balance—lay the groundwork for clean, accurate jewelry images. To elevate your photos to a truly professional level, you need advanced editing skills: seamless background removal, precise clipping paths, meticulous spot-healing, and targeted sharpening. These techniques allow you to isolate pieces, eliminate distractions, and emphasize fine details like metal textures and gemstone facets. In this chapter, you'll learn how to use industry-standard tools and non-destructive workflows to make every image pop without overprocessing.

Tools & Materials

- **Photo-editing Software**
    - Adobe Photoshop (with Pen tool, Layer Masks, Smart Objects)
    - Optional: Affinity Photo or GIMP for budget alternatives
- **Graphics Tablet** (e.g., Wacom) for precise hand-drawn selections
- **High-Resolution Source Files** (RAW or high-quality TIFFs)
- **Color-Checked and Calibrated Monitor** (see Chapter 10)
- **Custom Photoshop Actions or Scripts** for batch automation
- **Spot-Healing Brush and Clone Stamp Tools**
- **Layer Masking and Adjustment Layers** (to preserve non-destructive edits)
- **High-Pass Filter or Smart Sharpen** for selective sharpening

Step-by-Step Guide

1. **Prepare Your Document**

- Open your master TIFF or PSD file in Photoshop.
- Convert the background layer into a Smart Object to enable non-destructive transforms and filters.

2. **Create a Clipping Path**

   - Select the Pen tool; draw a precise path around your jewelry edge, zooming in to fine-tune anchor points.
   - Close the path, then right-click and choose "Make Selection" with a small feather radius (0.5–1 px) for smooth edges.
   - Save the path and convert it into a vector mask on your Smart Object layer.

3. **Refine Edge and Mask Cleanup**

   - With the vector mask selected, click "Select and Mask." Use the Refine Radius Brush to catch stray metal highlights or filigree.
   - Output to a layer mask; manually paint the mask with a soft brush to correct any remaining halos or jagged edges.

4. **Spot-Healing and Dust Removal**

   - Create a new blank layer above your image; set its blending mode to "Normal."
   - Use the Spot-Healing Brush Tool (Content-Aware) on that blank layer to remove dust specks and lint without altering original pixels.
   - Employ the Clone Stamp Tool sparingly on jewelry hallmarks or grooves, sampling nearby areas to maintain texture consistency.

5. **Background Enhancement or Replacement**

- With the jewelry isolated, add a solid-color or gradient fill layer underneath. Match the color to your branding palette.
- If using a custom textured backdrop (marble, wood), paste the texture layer below your masked jewelry and scale/position to suit.

6. **Selective Sharpening**
   - Convert your jewelry layer into a Smart Object if not already.
   - Apply a High-Pass filter (Radius: 1–2 px) set to "Overlay" blending to sharpen fine details.
   - Paint a white mask on the High-Pass layer and brush in sharpening only where needed—gemstone facets, metal edges—keeping surrounding areas soft.

7. **Color and Contrast Touch-Ups**
   - Add targeted Adjustment Layers (Curves, Hue/Saturation) clipped to the jewelry layer.
   - Use layer masks to confine adjustments to specific areas—brighten highlights on faceted gems without blowing out metal shine.

8. **Batch Automation**
   - Record a Photoshop Action that:
     - Converts to Smart Object
     - Applies clipping path mask
     - Runs High-Pass sharpening
     - Adds your default fill background layer

- Use File → Automate → Batch to apply this action to multiple files, then revisit each for custom spot fixes.

9. **Final Review and Export**

    - Inspect your composite at 100% zoom to catch any mask errors or over-sharpened halos.
    - Export as maximum-quality JPEG for web (sRGB) and archive a layered PSD or TIFF for future edits.

Tips & Tricks

- **Non-Destructive Workflow:** Always use Smart Objects and Adjustment Layers so you can revisit and tweak edits without image degradation.

- **Pen Tool Mastery:** Practice creating smooth Bézier curves; fewer anchor points yield more natural edges.

- **Mask Painting:** Switch between a hard-edged brush for clean lines and a soft brush for feathered transitions on metal highlights.

- **Action Variations:** Build multiple actions—one for white backgrounds, one for dark—to streamline different listing styles.

- **Edge Halos:** If you notice halos around your subject, slightly increase mask feather or manually blur mask edges by 0.3–0.5 px.

- **High-Pass Masking:** Invert your High-Pass mask to black and paint white only where sharpening enhances detail, avoiding noise in smooth areas.

- **Spot-Heal Layer:** Keeping spot-healing on its own layer lets you reduce opacity for subtler corrections.

- **Color Cast Artifacts:** After masking, check masked edges for residual color casts; use a small, low-flow brush and sample-neutral areas to clean up.

- **CPU Load Management:** Disable background saves and autosaves while running batch actions to speed up processing.

- **Archive Originals:** Always retain an unedited master copy so you can apply new techniques or branding changes later.

Chapter 12: Creating Branded Photo Templates

Overview

Templates accelerate your workflow and guarantee that every image in your Etsy shop looks cohesive and on-brand. By designing reusable layouts—with preset margins, image placeholders, and logo placement—you save time on repetitive tasks and maintain a polished, professional presentation. Whether you prefer Photoshop's power or Canva's simplicity, branded templates ensure consistent styling across product shots, promotional graphics, and social-media teasers.

Tools & Materials

- **Design Software**
    - Adobe Photoshop CC (with Smart Objects and Guides)
    - Canva Pro (Brand Kit enabled)

- **Brand Assets**
    - High-resolution logo (transparent PNG or SVG)
    - Color-palette swatches (hex codes)
    - Typography files (licensed fonts for headings and body text)

- **Sample Images**
    - A selection of your best raw or edited jewelry photos

- **Layout References**
    - Etsy image requirements (minimum 2000 px on the longest side)
    - Social-media aspect ratios (1:1 for Instagram, 4:5 for Pinterest)

- **Guidelines Document**

- One-page summary of margins, safe zones, and text hierarchy

Step-by-Step Guide

1. **Gather Brand Assets**

   - Create a folder named "Brand Kit" containing your logo files, color swatches, and font files.
   - Open your guidelines document so you can reference margins and safe-zone distances.

2. **Set Up a New Template Document**

   - In Photoshop, choose File → New.
     - Width: 2000 px, Height: 2000 px (square) or 2000 px × 2500 px (4:5).
     - Resolution: 300 dpi for print-quality exports; 72 dpi for purely digital use.
     - Color Mode: RGB.
   - In Canva, select "Custom Size," enter the same dimensions, and create a blank design.

3. **Define Safe Zones and Guides**

   - Photoshop: View → New Guide Layout →
     - Columns: 3 with 10 px gutters
     - Rows: 3 with 10 px gutters
     - Set margin guides of 150 px around edges.

- Canva: Enable "Show rulers and guides" and drag guides to 150 px from each edge.

4. **Create Image Placeholders**
   - Photoshop:
     - Draw a rectangle with the Rectangle Tool; convert it to a Smart Object placeholder (right-click → Convert to Smart Object).
     - Duplicate the Smart Object if you need multiple image slots (e.g., for flat-lay plus detail inset).
   - Canva:
     - Use "Frames" (Elements → Frames) and position one large frame with optional smaller inset frames.

5. **Add Brand Elements**
   - Import your logo; place it consistently in a corner (e.g., bottom right), sized no larger than 150 px tall.
   - Use your brand's headline font to add a text layer for product name—align it to the top guide line.
   - Add a secondary text placeholder ("Price • Material") using your body-text font, positioned 50 px below the headline.

6. **Incorporate Color Overlays (Optional)**
   - Photoshop: Create a new fill layer (Layer → New Fill Layer → Solid Color) with 10–20% opacity using your primary brand color.
   - Canva: Add a rectangle behind text, adjust transparency to 20%, and match your brand hex code.

7. **Build Export Presets**

    o Photoshop:

    - File → Export → Export As… → Save as JPEG, sRGB profile, Quality 80.
    - Save these settings as an export preset.

    o Canva:

    - Download settings: PNG or JPEG, compression slider at 80%.
    - Create a project template for future access.

8. **Test Your Template**

    o Replace Smart Object placeholders with sample jewelry images; ensure they scale and mask correctly.

    o Verify logo legibility and text contrast on light and dark pieces.

9. **Save and Organize**

    o Photoshop: Save as "Jewelry-Template.psd" in your Brand Kit folder.

    o Canva: Save as a project in your Brand Kit workspace and mark it as a template for your team.

10. **Duplicate for Additional Ratios**

    o Copy the master template file and adjust canvas size for square, vertical, and horizontal formats.

    o Reposition guides and placeholders to maintain safe zones and margins.

Tips & Tricks

- **Smart Objects for Flexibility:** Use Photoshop Smart Objects so you can update placeholders without losing masks or effects.

- **Canva Brand Kit:** Upload your fonts, logos, and colors once; every new template will automatically reflect your brand assets.

- **Consistent Spacing:** Use multiples of 10 px for margins and gutters to keep layouts tidy and grid-aligned.

- **Keyboard Shortcuts:** Learn shortcuts for copy/paste (⌘/Ctrl+C, ⌘/Ctrl+V), duplicate layer (⌘/Ctrl+J), and place embedded file (Shift + ⌘/Ctrl + P) for faster setup.

- **Group and Label Layers:** In Photoshop, group related layers (logo, text, image frames) and name them clearly for easy edits.

- **Version Control:** Keep dated versions (e.g., "Template_v1_2025-06.psd") so you can roll back if you try new layout ideas.

- **Batch Production:** In Photoshop, use File → Scripts → Image Processor to apply your template action to a folder of images.

- **Template Locking:** In Canva, lock guides and static elements so you don't accidentally move them while updating images.

- **Test on Multiple Devices:** Export a sample template and view on desktop and mobile to verify text readability and image scaling.

- **Document Your Workflow:** Save a one-page PDF walkthrough of how to update the template, so team members or future you can onboard quickly.

Chapter 13: Crafting Effective Listing Titles and Tags

Overview

An effective Etsy title and well-chosen tags help your jewelry listings surface in search results and connect with buyers' intent. The challenge is balancing high-value keywords with clear, engaging language that accurately represents your product. In this chapter, you'll learn how to research relevant search terms, structure titles for maximum visibility and readability, and select tags that capture both broad and niche shoppers—so your creations get found and clicked.

Tools & Materials

- **Keyword Research Tools**
    - Etsy search bar suggestions
    - eRank or Marmalead (free or paid tiers)

- **Spreadsheet or Table**
    - Columns for keyword, search volume, competition level, relevance

- **Competitor Analysis Notes**
    - Top-performing listings in your category (for inspiration)

- **Brand Voice Guidelines**
    - Tone (friendly, authoritative, whimsical) and key phrases from your brand statement

- **Character Counter**
    - Built-in Etsy title limit (140 characters) tracker

Step-by-Step Guide

1. **Gather Seed Keywords**

   - Type your product name into Etsy's search bar and note the autocomplete suggestions (e.g., "silver stacking rings," "dainty gold necklace").

   - Jot down 15–20 relevant phrases that match your piece's materials, style, or intended use.

2. **Analyze Keyword Metrics**

   - Enter seed keywords into your chosen research tool.

   - Record each term's approximate monthly search volume and competition score in your spreadsheet.

   - Flag keywords with high search volume and moderate-to-low competition for priority use.

3. **Identify Long-Tail Opportunities**

   - Look for 3- to 5-word phrases that describe unique features (e.g., "hand hammered silver cuff," "birthstone stacking ring set").

   - Long-tail keywords often convert better because they match specific buyer intent.

4. **Draft a Clear, Descriptive Title**

   - Begin with the primary keyword or phrase (highest priority term).

   - Follow with supporting descriptors: material, style, size, or intended recipient.

   - End with secondary keywords if space allows.

   - Example structure:

Primary Keyword · Material · Style/Feature · Recipient/Occasion · Secondary Keyword

"Sterling Silver Stacking Rings · Dainty Minimalist Bands · Bridal Jewelry Gift · Boho Stackable"

5. **Optimize for Readability**

   o Separate key phrases with commas or middle dots (·) to improve scanability.

   o Avoid keyword stuffing—ensure the title still reads like natural language.

   o Keep each phrase concise (2–4 words) so buyers can quickly understand what you're selling.

6. **Select Effective Tags**

   o Etsy allows up to 13 tags of 20 characters each.

   o Use all 13 slots.

   o Include:

   - Broad category (e.g., "earrings," "necklace")

   - Material (e.g., "rose gold," "gemstone")

   - Style (e.g., "boho," "vintage")

   - Occasion or recipient (e.g., "bridal gift," "mom jewelry")

   - Long-tail phrases (e.g., "stacking silver rings")

   o Avoid repeating words that are already in your title; tags should complement but not duplicate.

7. **Review and Refine**

- Read your title and tags together—ensure they cover all high-priority keywords without redundancy.
- Check character counts: titles max 140 characters, tags max 20 each.
- Preview how the first 75–100 characters of your title appear on mobile, where longer titles may be truncated.

8. **Implement in Your Listing**
   - Copy your optimized title and tags into Etsy's listing fields.
   - Save a clean version of your spreadsheet or keyword sheet for future listings and A/B testing.

9. **Monitor and Iterate**
   - After your listing goes live, track impressions and click-through rates in Etsy Shop Manager.
   - Identify terms that drive traffic and adjust underperforming tags or title phrases accordingly.
   - Repeat keyword research quarterly to stay current with trends and seasonal shifts.

Tips & Tricks

- **Use Synonyms and Regional Variants:** Include "jewellery" or "jewelry" if you sell internationally, but balance with your primary market's spelling.
- **Leverage Seasonal Keywords:** Add "Mother's Day gift" or "holiday stocking stuffer" tags several weeks before relevant events.
- **Group Keywords by Intent:** Organize your spreadsheet into "discovery" (broad) and "purchase" (specific) terms to guide title placement.

- **Avoid Filler Words:** Words like "beautiful," "nice," or "lovely" add little SEO value—reserve precious character space for keywords.

- **Test Two Title Variations:** Duplicate a listing and swap primary and secondary keywords between them; compare performance over a month.

- **Save Common Tags as a Template:** Create a reusable tag group in Etsy's "Saved Tags" feature for each product line to speed up listing creation.

- **Capitalize for Clarity:** Use title case or sentence case consistently; avoid ALL CAPS, which can feel spammy.

- **Monitor Competitor Shifts:** When top sellers tweak their titles or tags, review their changes for fresh keyword ideas.

- **Use Google Trends:** Validate high-volume Etsy terms against broader web searches to anticipate rising interest.

- **Document Tag Rationale:** Keep brief notes in your spreadsheet on why you chose each tag—this helps when you revisit or revise later.

Chapter 14: Writing Persuasive Product Descriptions

Tools & Materials

- **Product Specification Sheet**
  - Materials, dimensions, weight, finish, gemstone type, clasp style

- **Brand Voice Guide**
  - Key tone words, personality traits, approved phrases

- **Customer FAQs**
  - Real or anticipated questions about fit, durability, or care

- **Template Document**
  - Placeholder fields for each description element (opening, features, benefits, care)

- **Writing Notebook or Digital Notes App**
  - For brainstorming emotional hooks and benefit statements

Step-by-Step Guide

1. **Start with a Strong Opening**
   - Craft a one- or two-sentence hook that highlights the most desirable benefit or unique feature.
   - Example: "Elevate your everyday look with our hand-hammered sterling silver cuff, designed to catch the light and spark conversation."

2. **Detail Key Features Clearly**
   - List essential specifics: metal type and purity (e.g., 925 sterling silver), gemstone cut and carat weight, chain length, pendant dimensions.

- Keep each feature in its own brief sentence or phrase for skimmability.

3. **Translate Features into Buyer Benefits**
   - After each feature, explain why it matters:
     - "925 sterling silver—hypoallergenic and tarnish-resistant for everyday wear."
     - "Faceted emerald-cut stones—add timeless elegance and vibrant color to any outfit."

4. **Incorporate Sensory and Emotional Language**
   - Use descriptive adjectives that resonate with your audience's aspirations: "softly glowing," "boldly modern," "inspired by vintage heirlooms."
   - Invite the reader to imagine the experience: "Feel the warmth of gold plating against your skin as you step into evening gatherings."

5. **Address Common Questions and Objections**
   - Anticipate concerns about sizing, maintenance, or authenticity.
   - Provide concise answers: "Adjustable chain ensures the perfect fit from 16" to 18" necklaces" or "All gemstones are ethically sourced and hand-selected for clarity."

6. **Include Clear Care Instructions**
   - Offer straightforward guidance: "Wipe clean with a soft cloth; avoid water and chemicals to preserve shine."
   - Position care tips at the end of the description so buyers know how to maintain their investment.

7. **Add a Call-to-Action**

    o Conclude with an invitation: "Order today to add this versatile statement piece to your collection, or gift it to someone special."

    o Reinforce urgency or exclusivity if appropriate: "Limited edition—only 25 pieces available."

8. **Optimize for Readability and SEO**

    o Break text into short paragraphs (2–3 lines each).

    o Sprinkle primary and long-tail keywords naturally (e.g., "minimalist gold cuff," "handmade silver bracelet").

    o Use bullet points for feature/benefit pairs when space allows.

9. **Review and Refine**

    o Read aloud to catch awkward phrasing or redundancy.

    o Ensure consistency with your brand voice guide—tone, vocabulary, and sentence structure should align across all listings.

10. **Test Variations**

    o Try A/B testing two opening lines or benefit orders to see which yields higher click-through or conversion rates.

    o Update underperforming descriptions based on customer feedback and analytics.

Tips & Tricks

- **Lead with Benefits:** Always prioritize how a feature improves the wearer's life—comfort, confidence, style—before diving into technical details.

- **Use "You" Language:** Address the buyer directly ("You'll love how this ring…") to create a personal connection.

- **Keep It Scannable:** Bold or capitalize key terms sparingly (E.G., "HYPOALLERGENIC") to help skimmers spot important points.

- **Maintain Authenticity:** Avoid hyperbole—back claims with factual details to build trust.

- **Leverage Social Proof:** If you have endorsements or testimonials, quote a brief snippet in your description or a bullet ("'I've worn this every day!' – Sarah K.").

- **Seasonal Hooks:** Tie descriptions to upcoming events or gifting occasions: "A perfect Mother's Day surprise" or "Holiday party essential."

- **Character Limits:** Keep your primary description within the first 150–200 words so Etsy's mobile view shows the most compelling content before "Read more."

- **Highlight Scarcity or Exclusivity:** Words like "limited edition," "one-of-a-kind," or "handcrafted in small batches" can drive urgency.

- **Proofread Thoroughly:** Run your copy through a spell-checker and read backwards sentence by sentence to catch typos.

- **Document Best Practices:** Save top-performing descriptions as templates for new listings, adjusting only the specific details.

Chapter 15: Etsy SEO and Keyword Research

Overview

Effective Etsy SEO ensures that shoppers searching for jewelry find your listings first. By targeting high-traffic, relevant keywords—and integrating them organically into your titles, tags, and attributes—you boost your shop's visibility and attract qualified buyers. In this chapter, you'll learn how to use specialized tools to uncover valuable search terms, analyze their competitiveness, and apply insights to optimize every listing for maximum discoverability.

Tools & Materials

- **Etsy Search Bar** (for autocomplete suggestions)
- **SEO Research Platforms**
    - Marmalead
    - eRank
- **Supplemental Keyword Sources**
    - Google Trends
    - Google Keyword Planner (for broader market insights)
- **Spreadsheet or Keyword Tracker** (Google Sheets, Excel)
- **Competitor Audit Notes** (top sellers in your niche)
- **Listing Drafts** (to test optimized titles and tags)

Step-by-Step Guide

1. **Collect Seed Terms**

- Enter your product's core descriptors into the Etsy search bar and note autocomplete suggestions (e.g., "dainty gold necklace," "boho beaded bracelet").
- List at least 15–20 foundational phrases in your spreadsheet.

2. **Expand with SEO Tools**

    - Input seed terms into Marmalead or eRank.
    - Gather data on monthly search volume, engagement scores, and competition levels for each term.

3. **Analyze and Prioritize Keywords**

    - Highlight keywords with high search volume and moderate-to-low competition.
    - Flag long-tail phrases (3–5 words) that capture specific buyer intent (e.g., "adjustable stacking rings set").

4. **Map Keywords to Listing Elements**

    - Assign your strongest primary keyword to the beginning of the title.
    - Distribute secondary and long-tail keywords across remaining title slots and tags.
    - Populate Etsy's attribute fields (e.g., "Metal," "Stone," "Style") with matching terms to reinforce relevance.

5. **Optimize Tag Selection**

    - Use all 13 tag slots.

- Include a mix of broad (e.g., "necklace") and niche (e.g., "moonstone pendant") terms.
- Avoid repeating words already in the title—tags should complement, not duplicate.

6. **Leverage Categories and Attributes**
    - Choose the most accurate category path (e.g., Jewelry → Necklaces → Pendant Necklaces).
    - Fill in every relevant attribute (color, material, recipient) to tap into Etsy's filtered search.

7. **Draft and Compare Variations**
    - Create two versions of your title and tag set in your spreadsheet.
    - Reference competitor bestsellers to see what's performing well and where gaps exist.

8. **Implement and Monitor**
    - Update your listing with the optimized title, tags, and attributes.
    - In Etsy Shop Manager, track impressions, clicks, and conversion rates over 2–4 weeks.

9. **Refine Based on Data**
    - Identify keywords bringing high impressions but low clicks—experiment with more descriptive titles or stronger calls-to-action.
    - Drop underperforming tags and swap in new long-tail terms from your keyword tracker.

10. **Schedule Regular Reviews**
    - Set a quarterly calendar reminder to revisit keyword data, account for seasonality, and refresh listings.
    - Keep your spreadsheet up to date with emerging trends (holiday gifts, birthstones, style movements).

Tips & Tricks

- **Seasonal Surge Planning:** Monitor Google Trends for spikes in terms like "Mother's Day jewelry" or "Christmas stocking stuffer" and preemptively update listings.

- **Regional Spelling Variations:** If you ship internationally, consider alternate spellings ("jewellery" vs. "jewelry") in tags—without overloading your title.

- **Use Synonyms:** Broaden reach by tagging synonyms: "gemstone" and "stone," "stacking" and "stackable."

- **Attribute Synergy:** When you select a material attribute (e.g., "sterling silver"), Etsy automatically applies related search filters—capitalize on this.

- **Stay Out of "Banned Words":** Avoid prohibited terms (e.g., "guarantee," "free shipping") that Etsy may suppress or flag.

- **Competitor Cross-Checking:** Periodically scan top-selling competitor listings to spot newly popular keywords or phrasing.

- **Test Early, Test Often:** New listings may rank temporarily higher; use this "freshness" period to gauge which keywords stick.

- **Character-Cautious Tagging:** Tags truncate at 20 characters—use concise, high-impact phrases (e.g., "minimalist ring").

- **Batch Updates:** When refining, update 5–10 listings at a time to measure changes without destabilizing your entire shop's SEO.

- **Document Learnings:** Maintain a "SEO Playbook" sheet in your tracker with notes on what worked and why—with dates—so you build institutional knowledge.

Chapter 16: Pricing Strategies and Inventory Planning

Overview

Getting your pricing right and managing inventory effectively are key to sustaining a profitable Etsy shop. Price too low, and you erode your margins; price too high, and you deter buyers. Overstock or understock, and you tie up capital or miss sales. In this chapter, you'll learn how to calculate true product costs, apply healthy profit margins, research competitive prices, and establish inventory workflows—so you can price confidently and keep stock levels optimized for demand.

Tools & Materials

- **Cost-Calculator Spreadsheet**
- **Competitor Price Audit Sheet** (spreadsheet or table)
- **Inventory Tracker** (Google Sheets, Excel, or dedicated app)
- **Production Time Log** (notebook or digital timer)
- **Shipping-Cost Reference** (rate charts from USPS, UPS, etc.)
- **Raw-Material Price List** (updated regularly)
- **Sales-Forecast Template**

Step-by-Step Guide

1. **Calculate Total Cost per Unit**

    - **Materials:** Sum the costs of metals, gemstones, findings, and packaging per piece.
    - **Labor:** Record time spent crafting one unit and multiply by your target hourly rate.

- **Overhead:** Allocate a percentage for utilities, tools depreciation, marketing, and Etsy fees.
- Enter these figures into your cost-calculator spreadsheet to derive a "break-even" cost.

2. **Research Market Prices**
   - Audit 5–10 similar Etsy listings: note their prices, materials, and craftsmanship levels.
   - Record low, median, and high prices in your audit sheet to understand your competitive range.

3. **Set Your Profit Margin**
   - Decide on a target margin (e.g., 40–60%).
   - Apply margin:

     - Price = Cost ÷ (1 – Margin %)
   - Round prices strategically (e.g., $48.99 instead of $50) to align with buyer psychology.

4. **Incorporate Shipping and Fees**
   - Factor in average shipping costs—consider offering free shipping by building the cost into your price.
   - Account for Etsy transaction and payment-processing fees (typically 6–8%).
   - Update your price formula accordingly to preserve margin.

5. **Implement Tiered Pricing (Optional)**

- Offer volume discounts or bundle sets (e.g., buy two, get 10% off).
- Ensure tiered pricing still covers your break-even cost plus margin.

6. **Build Your Inventory Plan**
   - Use sales-history data or seasonal forecasts to set reorder points (e.g., replenish when stock hits five units).
   - Batch production: schedule crafting in blocks to reduce setup time and material waste.
   - Track each SKU: record on-hand quantities, production dates, and materials on order.

7. **Monitor and Adjust**
   - Review actual sales, costs, and profit monthly.
   - Update material prices and labor rates in your calculator to reflect changes.
   - Adjust prices or batch sizes if you notice stockouts or slow-moving items.

8. **Maintain Safety Stock**
   - Keep a small buffer (e.g., 10–20% above forecasted demand) to absorb sudden order spikes or supply delays.

Tips & Tricks

- **Use Conditional Formatting:** In your spreadsheet, highlight SKUs below the reorder point in red for immediate attention.
- **Leverage Etsy Stats:** Identify best-selling items and focus inventory on top performers.

- **Automate Alerts:** Set calendar reminders or app notifications for reorder dates based on your tracker.

- **Bundle Materials Purchases:** Order raw materials in larger quantities to secure volume discounts and reduce per-unit cost.

- **Review Costs Quarterly:** Raw-material prices fluctuate—update your cost models every three months.

- **Test Price Increments:** Increase prices in small increments (5–10%) to gauge buyer sensitivity without drastic sales drop-offs.

- **Offer Limited Editions:** Create small runs of special pieces to stimulate urgency and clear older stock.

- **Track WIP (Work in Progress):** Record items mid-production to avoid double-counting and to plan your crafting schedule accurately.

- **Plan for Returns:** Allocate a small percentage (e.g., 2–3%) of stock for potential returns or defects.

- **Keep a Profit Dashboard:** Visualize revenue, costs, and margins in a simple chart to spot trends and make data-driven decisions.

Chapter 17: Shop Branding and Visual Identity

Overview

A cohesive visual identity instills confidence in shoppers and strengthens recall across every touchpoint—from your Etsy banner to your social-media posts. Consistent use of logos, colors, and typography signals professionalism and makes browsing your shop a seamless experience. In this chapter, you'll learn how to design and implement strong brand assets—shop banners, icons, product badges, and more—to reinforce your brand story and build trust.

Tools & Materials

- **Design Software**
    - Adobe Illustrator or Photoshop (for vector logos and layered banners)
    - Canva Pro (for templated, drag-and-drop designs)

- **Brand Kit Folder**
    - Logo files (vector SVG, transparent-PNG)
    - Color-palette swatches (hex/RGB codes)
    - Typography files (web-safe or licensed fonts)

- **Etsy Asset Specifications**
    - Shop banner: 1200 × 300 px (min 1200 × 160 px)
    - Logo/icon: 500 × 500 px
    - Listing thumbnails: 2000 px on longest side

- **Social-Media Templates**
    - Instagram post (1080 × 1080 px), story (1080 × 1920 px)

- Pinterest pin (1000 × 1500 px)
- **Mood Board** (from Chapter 2)
- **Notebook or Digital Sketchpad**

Step-by-Step Guide

1. **Revisit Your Brand Guide**
   - Open your one-page brand statement, color codes, and font choices.
   - Confirm the vibe keywords (e.g., "modern minimal," "rustic boho") you want to express visually.

2. **Design Your Logo/Icon**
   - Sketch or import existing symbols that reflect your brand essence (moon phases, floral motifs, geometric lines).
   - Create a simple, scalable logo: focus on clear shapes that read well at 50 px and 500 px.
   - Export as SVG for crisp web display and PNG with transparent background for versatility.

3. **Create Your Shop Banner**
   - In Illustrator or Canva, set canvas to 1200 × 300 px.
   - Apply your primary brand color as background or a subtle gradient.
   - Place your logo on the left third, leaving negative space for shop name and tagline.
   - Add concise text: shop name in headline font; tagline or value proposition in body font.

- Save two versions: full banner and mobile-optimized (cropped to 1200 × 160 px).

4. **Develop Supporting Graphics**
   - **Section Dividers:** 800 × 200 px PNGs or SVGs for "About," "FAQs," and "Policies" pages.
   - **Product Badges:** Circular icons (e.g., "Handmade," "Eco-Friendly," "Limited Edition") sized 200 × 200 px.
   - **Social-Media Templates:**
     - Create a 1080 × 1080 px Instagram post template with a reserved photo area and branded frame.
     - Design a 1080 × 1920 px story template with space for text overlays and call-to-action.

5. **Implement on Etsy**
   - Upload your banner and logo in Shop Settings → Info & Appearance.
   - Add section-divider images under Shop Manager → Shop Sections.
   - Apply product badges as listing icons using "Production Partner" fields or image overlays in templates.

6. **Apply Across Channels**
   - Use your social-media templates to announce new products, sales, or behind-the-scenes peeks.
   - Ensure your Etsy "About" page features your banner and consistent typography for headings and body text.

- Link your Etsy shop from Instagram and Pinterest bios, using your logo as the profile image.

7. **Review for Consistency**
    - Browse your shop on desktop and mobile to confirm text legibility, image alignment, and color fidelity.
    - Ask a friend or colleague to navigate your pages and provide feedback on clarity and visual appeal.

8. **Iterate and Update**
    - Schedule a bi-annual brand-review session.
    - Refresh seasonal elements (e.g., holiday banners) while maintaining core brand colors and fonts.
    - Archive previous assets for reference and to track brand evolution.

Tips & Tricks

- **Grid Alignment:** Use a 3-column grid when designing banners to position logo, text, and CTA evenly.

- **Font Pairing:** Pair a distinctive display font for your shop name with a highly legible sans-serif for body text.

- **Consistent Corners:** If you use rounded corners on thumbnails or badges, apply the same radius across all assets.

- **Contrast Check:** Confirm text meets WCAG contrast ratios against your background colors for accessibility.

- **Template Locking:** In Canva, lock your logo and color blocks so you only swap images or update text.

- **Save Brand Kit in Cloud:** Store your Brand Kit folder in Dropbox or Google Drive for access across devices.

- **Use Mockups:** Place your logo on free digital mockups (coffee mug, tote bag) to visualize future merchandise.

- **Brand Watermark:** Add a semi-transparent version of your logo to listing thumbnails to deter image theft.

- **Mobile-First Design:** Always preview social-media and Etsy assets on a phone before finalizing.

- **Document File Naming:** Name files descriptively (e.g., "Banner_Main_2025_v1.png") to avoid confusion during updates.

Chapter 18: Promoting Your Listings on Social Media

Overview

Social media platforms like Instagram, Facebook, and Pinterest are powerful channels to showcase your jewelry, engage potential customers, and drive traffic to your Etsy shop. By creating a mix of static posts, short-form videos, and story content that highlights your design process and finished pieces, you build an authentic connection and boost discoverability. This chapter shows you how to plan, produce, and schedule shareable content that aligns with your brand aesthetic and converts followers into buyers.

Tools & Materials

- **Smartphone or Camera** capable of shooting high-resolution photos and video (1080p or higher)

- **Tripod or Gimbal** for stable video reels and time-lapses

- **Lighting** (natural window light or portable LED panel)

- **Editing Apps**

    o Photos: Lightroom Mobile, VSCO

    o Video: InShot, CapCut, Adobe Premiere Rush

- **Content Calendar** (spreadsheet or a scheduling tool like Later, Buffer, or Planoly)

- **Graphic Templates** (from Chapter 13's Canva or Photoshop assets)

- **Hashtag Research Tool** (e.g., Display Purposes, RiteTag)

- **Analytics Dashboard** (native Instagram/Facebook Insights or a third-party tool)

Step-by-Step Guide

1. **Define Your Content Pillars**

- Choose 3–4 themes (e.g., product showcases, behind the scenes, styling tips, customer testimonials).
- Allocate a percentage of posts to each pillar (e.g., 40% showcases, 30% BTS, 20% tips, 10% UGC).

2. **Plan a Weekly Schedule**
   - Use a content calendar to map posts: static images on Mondays, reels on Wednesdays, stories daily.
   - Align posts with promotions, holidays, and new launches for maximum relevance.

3. **Shoot Static Product Posts**
   - Frame jewelry on your branded backdrop (see Chapter 7) using consistent lighting and composition.
   - Capture multiple angles: full piece, detail close-up, styled flat-lay.
   - Edit to your template's aspect ratio (1:1 for Instagram feed, 4:5 for Facebook).

4. **Create Engaging Reels and Video**
   - Plan short videos (15–30 seconds) showing unboxing, jewelry on-model, or styling sequences.
   - Use a tripod or gimbal to keep footage smooth; incorporate quick cuts and trending music.
   - Include text overlays for calls-to-action ("Tap to shop," "Link in bio").

5. **Document Behind-the-Scenes**

- Share time-lapses of your setup (lighting changes, prop arrangements), close-ups of crafting, or packing orders.
- Keep clips under 20 seconds for stories or 60 seconds for feed videos.
- Add captions or narration explaining techniques or inspiration.

6. **Design Pinterest Pins**

    - Create vertical pins (1000 × 1500 px) using your branded templates and lifestyle imagery.
    - Overlay clear text titles ("How to Style a Layered Necklace," "Handcrafted Silver Ring Care").
    - Link each pin directly to the relevant Etsy listing or a blog post.

7. **Write Captions and Hashtags**

    - Pair each post with a concise, benefit-driven caption (e.g., "Our hammered gold cuff adds subtle texture to any outfit—shop now!").
    - Research 10–15 relevant hashtags—mix popular (#jewelryforsale) with niche (#bohojewelrydesigner).
    - Place hashtags after a line break or in the first comment to keep captions clean.

8. **Schedule and Automate**

    - Use a scheduling tool to queue posts at optimal engagement times (based on your analytics).
    - Pre-load captions, hashtags, and first comments; enable reminders for stories or live sessions.

9. **Engage and Respond**
    - Reply to comments and DMs within 24 hours.
    - Encourage user-generated content by asking customers to tag you when they wear your jewelry.
    - Repost customer photos as social proof (with permission).
10. **Analyze and Refine**
    - Review post-performance weekly: impressions, saves, shares, click-throughs to your Etsy link.
    - Identify top-performing formats (e.g., reels vs. static) and pillars, then adjust your content mix accordingly.

Tips & Tricks

- **Batch Shoot:** Dedicate one day to filming and photographing for the entire week—maximizing efficiency.
- **Use Templates:** Leverage your branded Canva or Photoshop layouts to maintain consistency and speed up design.
- **Trending Audio:** Incorporate current popular songs in reels to increase reach via algorithmic boosts.
- **Pinning Strategy:** Pin both your content and relevant evergreen pins daily to grow Pinterest visibility.
- **Story Highlights:** Save key BTS, tutorials, and customer reviews in Highlights on Instagram for new followers to browse.
- **Cross-Promote:** Share your Instagram reels to Facebook and TikTok, tailoring formats as needed.

- **Geo-Tagging and Tagging:** Tag your location and relevant accounts (e.g., material suppliers) to expand discoverability.

- **Micro-Influencers:** Partner with small-scale influencers (under 10K followers) for shout-outs or styling collaborations.

- **Educational Carousels:** Create swipeable posts explaining care tips or styling ideas for higher engagement.

- **Regular Refresh:** Update your content calendar monthly to align with holidays, seasons, and new product drops.

Chapter 19: Tracking Performance and Scaling Your Business

Overview

Ongoing growth requires more than beautiful photos and optimized listings—you need data-driven insights and strategic planning. By regularly monitoring key performance indicators (KPIs), testing new approaches, and expanding thoughtfully, you can scale your jewelry business sustainably. This chapter teaches you how to interpret Etsy and external analytics, set measurable goals, run simple experiments, and leverage partnerships or outsourcing so your shop continues to thrive as demand grows.

Tools & Materials

- **Etsy Shop Manager Analytics** (Impressions, Visits, Conversion Rate, Revenue)
- **Google Analytics** (for Etsy shops with external domains or a linked website)
- **Spreadsheet or Dashboard** (Google Sheets, Airtable, or dedicated BI tool)
- **Key Performance Indicator Template** (monthly tracking of KPIs)
- **A/B Testing Plan Worksheet** (hypothesis, variant details, test duration)
- **Email Marketing Platform** (Mailchimp, Klaviyo, or similar)
- **Outsourcing Directory** (Upwork, Fiverr, local craft assistants)
- **Inventory and Production Forecasting Template**

Step-by-Step Guide

1. **Define Your Core KPIs**
    - Impressions (how often your listings appear)
    - Click-through Rate (CTR: visits ÷ impressions)
    - Conversion Rate (sales ÷ visits)

- Average Order Value (AOV)
- Customer Acquisition Cost (total marketing spend ÷ number of buyers)
- Repeat Purchase Rate

2. **Set Up a Monthly Tracking System**
   - Create a spreadsheet with columns for each KPI and rows for each month.
   - Record baseline numbers for the past three months to establish trends.

3. **Analyze Analytics Regularly**
   - Review Etsy's "Shop Stats" weekly for fluctuations in traffic sources (search, social, direct).
   - Use Google Analytics to track off-Etsy traffic, bounce rates, and new vs. returning visitors.

4. **Identify Opportunities and Bottlenecks**
   - Low impressions? Revisit SEO, tags, and ad spend.
   - High visits but low conversion? Test listing images, descriptions, or pricing.
   - Declining AOV? Implement upsell bundles, free-shipping thresholds, or volume discounts.

5. **Craft A/B Tests**
   - Choose one variable at a time (e.g., main product image, headline phrasing, price point).
   - Divide traffic evenly (via two separate but identical listings or external landing pages).

- Run each test for at least two sales cycles (e.g., two weeks or until 50 conversions).
- Compare conversion rates and statistically significant differences.

6. **Scale Winning Variants**
    - Apply successful image styles or description formats across your top-selling listings.
    - Increase ad spend or promote star products on social media using proven creative assets.

7. **Leverage Email Marketing**
    - Build an email list via a newsletter signup on your website or Etsy Shop Updates.
    - Send regular campaigns featuring new releases, restocks, and exclusive discounts.
    - Track email-driven revenue in your spreadsheet to calculate return on investment.

8. **Plan for Inventory Growth**
    - Forecast demand based on seasonal trends and A/B test outcomes.
    - Schedule production blocks, factoring in lead times for materials—use your production forecasting template.
    - Maintain safety stock for bestsellers to prevent stockouts.

9. **Consider Outsourcing and Partnerships**

- Delegate repetitive tasks—packaging, order fulfillment, photo editing—to virtual assistants or local helpers.
- Partner with complementary brands (e.g., gift-box makers) for joint promotions or bundled offerings.
- Monitor the cost-benefit of outsourcing to ensure it enhances margins.

10. **Review, Adjust, and Repeat**
    - At month's end, compare actual KPI changes against targets.
    - Document key learnings in a "Business Growth Journal."
    - Refine goals, tests, and resource allocations for the next cycle.

Tips & Tricks

- **Visual Dashboards:** Use spreadsheet charts or free BI tools to graph trends—visual cues help spot issues quickly.
- **Micro-Goals:** Break annual revenue targets into monthly or weekly milestones to maintain focus.
- **Automate Data Collection:** Where possible, connect your Etsy shop to Zapier or Integromat to auto-update your tracking spreadsheet.
- **Customer Surveys:** Send brief post-purchase surveys to gauge satisfaction and collect ideas for product expansions.
- **Loyalty Incentives:** Reward repeat customers with discount codes to boost your repeat purchase rate KPI.
- **Referral Programs:** Encourage word-of-mouth by offering small perks to customers who refer friends.

- **Seasonal Prep:** Analyze prior-year data to plan promotions and inventory six weeks before peak seasons like holidays.

- **Time-Blocking:** Dedicate a fixed hour each week exclusively for analytics review and decision-making.

- **Outsource Selectively:** Start by outsourcing one non-core task (e.g., bookkeeping) and scale up as ROI becomes clear.

- **Document Everything:** Keep records of every test variant, inventory decision, and partnership outcome to build institutional memory.

The end

Printed in Dunstable, United Kingdom